ESFP: BEYOND THE SPOTLIGHT

Your Guide to Endless Adventure

Asa Eccleston Kibilski

CONTENTS

THE MASK OF THE ENTERTAINER

Beneath the Laughter: Understanding the ESFP's Social Persona

The world sees the ESFP as a dazzling social butterfly, flitting from one exciting moment to the next, spreading laughter and infectious enthusiasm. The spotlight always seems to find them, and they appear to thrive in its warmth. They are the life of the party, the ones with a smile on their face and a witty quip on their lips. It's as if they exist purely to entertain, putting on a performance everyone else enjoys.

But like any good performer, the ESFP holds a secret: the person they present to the world is often a carefully constructed mask. This doesn't imply dishonesty; rather, the "Entertainer" persona is often a defense mechanism, protection crafted out of necessity. The ESFP is wired for connection and deeply sensitive to the emotions of those around them. This social mask allows the ESFP a degree of control in a chaotic world, shielding them from the weight of others' expectations.

Think of the classic court jester. Their outlandish costumes, silly antics, and sharp wit offered a form of entertainment that made even harsh truths easier to swallow. The ESFP similarly adopts a performative nature to navigate social situations. It's both a way to put people at ease and to maintain a sense of emotional distance. They entertain to deflect, they charm to disarm.

The ESFP's core drive is to connect with others and create a joyous, vibrant experience. Their natural ability to read a room and sense what people need fuels their social talents. Whether it's a well-timed joke to break tension, a genuine compliment that makes someone's day, or throwing an impromptu dance party just because, the ESFP intuitively knows how to uplift those around them.

This outward focus is a tremendous gift, but it can easily become a crutch. If all their energy is directed toward entertaining others, what remains for themselves? The constant need to perform can become exhausting, a drain on the energy an ESFP craves. This is why you'll often see the ESFP suddenly withdraw after a period of intense social interaction. They need to recharge, to shed the mask momentarily before they can re-enter the spotlight.

The ESFP's need for attention and validation sometimes gets mislabeled as shallowness. It's vital to understand that this comes from their deep-seated craving for genuine connection. They want to feel seen, appreciated, and loved for who they are, not just the entertainment they provide. The problem is, the ESFP's social mask can make genuine connection feel elusive. How do you truly know a person who seems so dedicated to the performance?

Key takeaways from this section:

- The ESFP's "Entertainer" persona is both a blessing and a challenge.
- This social mask serves a purpose: it allows the ESFP to control social interactions and protect their sensitive nature.
- The ESFP's innate talent is in creating positive, joyful experiences for others.
- The relentless need for attention and validation arises from a desire for genuine connection.

When the Applause Fades: Dealing with Loneliness

The applause dies down, the party ends, and the spotlight switches off. The ESFP is left alone with their own reflection, the mask of the Entertainer no longer serving its purpose. It's in these quiet moments, when the external stimulation fades, that a pervasive sense of loneliness can creep in. The contrast between the vibrancy of their social life and the emptiness felt afterward can be stark.

This loneliness isn't necessarily about lacking people around them. ESFPs often have a wide network of friends and acquaintances. The loneliness is an internal one, a sense of disconnection from their true selves. The ESFP, having spent so much energy crafting their social image, can lose sight of who they are beneath that facade. It becomes frighteningly easy to mistake external validation for an internal sense of worth.

The fear of solitude is a significant issue for many ESFPs. It's not just about not wanting to be alone, it's about confronting uncomfortable emotions they've skillfully kept at bay. Silence amplifies fears they've carefully danced around: the fear of rejection, the fear of not being enough, the fear of being left behind.

Distraction becomes a survival tool. They might fill every moment with activities, chase the next thrill, or seek out the company of others to avoid the nagging question: "If I strip away the persona, will anyone still love me?"

This fear of being seen extends to deeper vulnerability. The ESFP might worry that showing sadness, anger, or insecurity will tarnish their image or burden others. Laughter becomes their default, even when inappropriate. Yet, bottling up these emotions only makes them more potent.

The ESFP's loneliness is a paradox. They are surrounded by people they care about, yet they feel a profound sense of isolation. This disconnect arises from the inability to form authentic connections when they themselves don't feel fully known or accepted. They crave intimacy but fear opening themselves up completely, lest they disappoint those who have grown accustomed to their lighthearted persona.

Key takeaways from this section:

- The ESFP's loneliness stems from internal disconnection rather than a lack of social interaction.
- The fear of silence and solitude arises from the fear of confronting suppressed emotions.

- The ESFP's "always on" energy can be a way to avoid vulnerability and deeper intimacy.
- The constant need to be the center of attention can hinder the formation of truly authentic connections.

SENSATIONAL LIVING

The Thrill of the Moment: Embracing the Present

ESFPs are masters of living in the moment. Their dominant cognitive function, Extroverted Sensing (Se), gives them an almost unparalleled ability to fully engage with the sensory world. They notice the vibrant colors, the subtle textures, the intoxicating smells, and the intricate details that others often miss. The present moment becomes a feast for their senses, and they delight in savoring every bite.

Think of a child completely absorbed in play, lost in a world of their own creation. There's a purity in that focused attention, an ability to block out distractions and just *be*. ESFPs possess a similar childlike wonder, even as adults, allowing them to find immense joy in simple experiences. Whether it's the first sip of morning coffee, the feel of cool grass beneath bare feet, or the explosion of color at a street festival, ESFPs have a knack for being fully present.

This ability to live in the "now" is both a gift and a challenge. On the positive side, ESFPs are rarely held back by regrets about the past or anxieties about the future. They have a remarkable talent for letting go and embracing what is right in front of them. This makes them spontaneous, adaptable, and incredibly resilient. When life throws them a curveball, they are often the first to find the silver lining and adapt to the new situation, rather than dwell on what might have been.

ESFPs understand that life is fleeting, and their desire to fully experience everything can create a sense of urgency. They have an unquenchable thirst for novelty and adventure. Their ideal world is a never-ending playground of sensory delights, where no two days are ever the same.

Key takeaways from this section:

- ESFPs have an exceptional ability to fully engage with the present moment through their senses.
- Their focus on the "here-and-now" allows them to find joy in everyday experiences.
- ESFPs are adaptable and resilient, able to move on from setbacks quickly.
- Their desire to make the most of every moment fuels their adventurous spirit.

Craving the Extraordinary: When Normal Isn't Enough

The ESFP's zest for life makes the ordinary feel mundane. They have a deep-seated aversion to routine and predictability. While others may find comfort in the familiar, the ESFP craves the pulse-quickening rush of the new and the unexpected. This desire for the extraordinary can lead them on fantastic adventures, but it can also cause discontent if their environment becomes too predictable.

Imagine a vibrant butterfly being forced to live within a small, drab box. That's how an ESFP feels when confined to a monotonous routine. Their spirit yearns for more than the 9-to-5 workday, the same meals every week, or the endless scroll of humdrum tasks. They want to paint their life with bold colors, to try flavors they've never tasted, and to dance to rhythms they've never heard.

This thirst for the unconventional often leads ESFPs to try new hobbies, explore new places, and jump at spontaneous opportunities. They have a boundless curiosity about the world and a belief that there's always something exciting just around the corner. The problem arises when their environment cannot keep pace with their need for constant stimulation.

Boredom is the ESFP's kryptonite. It can drive them to restless frustration and even reckless behavior as they seek an escape from the unbearable feeling of being "stuck." Trapped in a stagnant situation, they become prone to impulsive decisions or self-sabotaging behavior just to create some form of change, even if that change isn't necessarily positive.

The key for ESFPs is to find a balance. They need outlets for their adventurous spirit, a way to channel their craving for the extraordinary into productive and fulfilling pursuits. Whether it's travel, trying new sports, taking on creative projects, or simply shaking up their daily routines, they need spaces to explore, experiment, and feel their spirit take flight.

Key takeaways from this section:

- ESFPs have a powerful dislike for routine and crave novel, stimulating experiences.
- Boredom can be extremely demotivating and even destructive for an ESFP.
- ESFPs thrive on change, exploration, and pursuing their passions.
- Finding healthy ways to fulfill their need for excitement is crucial to their well-being.

The challenge for the ESFP is to learn how to satisfy that thirst for the extraordinary without leading a chaotic or unfulfilling life. This exploration might be part of the next chapter!

RELATIONSHIP RHAPSODY

Connecting with Heart: The Power of ESFP Empathy

ESFPs are often described as social butterflies, but their connections with others run far deeper than mere surface-level charm. At their core, ESFPs possess a profound capacity for empathy that makes them exceptional friends, partners, and confidants. They have an innate ability to tune into the emotions of others, sensing unspoken joy, hidden sorrow, and the myriad of complex feelings in between.

This heartfelt empathy is born from the ESFPs strong Extroverted Feeling (Fe) function. They are deeply attuned to the emotional atmosphere of any situation and can pick up on subtle cues others might miss. It's as if they have a sixth sense for the emotional needs of those around them. An ESFP will notice a forced smile, a tremble in a friend's voice, or a flicker of sadness in someone's usually bright eyes.

Their empathy is not just passive observation. ESFPs have a powerful urge to act on their understanding of others' emotions. They want to make people feel seen, heard, and valued. Whether it's an enthusiastic celebration of a friend's success, a shoulder to cry on during a difficult time, or a perfectly timed pep-talk to boost someone's confidence, ESFPs have a way of offering just the right kind of support.

Think of the ESFP as an emotional mirror, reflecting back the feelings of those around them while adding their own warmth and optimism. They are often the ones people turn to when they need validation, comfort, or an extra dose of courage. The very presence of an ESFP can be healing for those struggling with difficult emotions.

The gift of ESFP empathy comes from a place of genuine care and concern. Their focus isn't just on what someone says but how that person feels. They have the remarkable ability to step into someone else's shoes and see the world through their eyes, which fosters deep understanding and a genuine desire to help.

Key Takeaways from this Section:

- ESFPs have a strong capacity for empathy, making them deeply attuned to the emotions of others.
- This empathy stems from their focus on the emotional well-being of those around them.
- ESFPs often act as an emotional mirror, reflecting understanding and adding warmth.
- Their ability to make people feel seen and heard creates deep and lasting connections.

Needing the Spotlight: Love, Validation & Codependency

The ESFP's gift of empathy and their desire to make others feel loved can become a double-edged sword. Their deep need for connection and affirmation, coupled with their natural inclination to put the needs of others first, can lead to unhealthy patterns of codependency in relationships.

Craving the spotlight in relationships is a paradox faced by many ESFPs. On one hand, they bask in the warmth of positive attention, their self-esteem intrinsically linked to the approval they receive. On the other hand, their deep love for others can overshadow their own emotional needs.

This leads to seeking external validation as a primary means of feeling good about themselves. If their partner, friend, or family member expresses affection, admiration, or gratitude, the ESFP feels worthy and loved. But the reverse is also true. Any perceived withdrawal of affection, even minor criticism, can have a disproportionate effect on their emotional well-being.

Codependency in an ESFP often manifests as:

- People-pleasing: Going to extreme lengths to make others

happy, even to their own detriment.

- Loss of identity: Their sense of self becomes intertwined with that of their partner or friend.
- Difficulty setting boundaries: They feel responsible for the emotions of others and struggle to say "no."
- Fear of abandonment: They desperately try to hold onto relationships, even if they are unhealthy.

Codependent tendencies in ESFPs can stem from past experiences where their own needs were neglected, leading them to believe love must be earned. It's also common for the highly empathetic ESFP to absorb the emotions of those close to them, becoming entangled in someone else's problems and losing sight of who they are outside of that dynamic.

The challenge for the ESFP is to recognize their self-worth without needing constant external validation. This involves developing a healthy sense of self-love and learning to prioritize their own emotional needs alongside those of their loved ones.

Key Takeaways from this Section:

- ESFPs' deep need for love and validation can make them vulnerable to codependent relationships.
- They may become people-pleasers and lose their sense of self in an effort to be loved.
- Codependent ESFPs often struggle with boundaries and fear abandonment.
- Prioritizing self-love and understanding their own emotional needs is essential to break codependent patterns.

Understanding this dynamic is crucial for an ESFP. The path to healthy, balanced relationships begins with recognizing where their desire for connection turns into a need for someone else to complete them.

THE SENSITIVE SOUL

Unexpected Vulnerability: Handling Criticism & Rejection

Beneath the ESFP's bright and cheerful exterior lies a surprising depth of feeling. While they often put on a brave face and try to keep things light, ESFPs are deeply sensitive individuals who can be profoundly affected by criticism, disappointment, and rejection.

The source of this sensitivity lies in their auxiliary function - Introverted Feeling (Fi). While they focus on the emotional world of others (through the lens of their dominant Extroverted Sensing), they still possess a strong sense of personal values and internal emotions. This Fi function often remains hidden, but that doesn't lessen its impact.

ESFPs take great pride in being loved and admired. Their self-image is closely tied to how they believe others perceive them. When they face negative feedback or feel that someone disapproves of them, it cuts deeper than it might appear on the surface. This can lead to a number of defense mechanisms:

- Deflecting with humor: An ESFP might crack a joke or dismiss criticism to avoid dealing with the hurt feelings underneath.
- Withdrawing: They might retreat from social interaction, needing time to process their emotions in private.
- Lashing out: Sometimes, the hurt manifests as anger, where they blame others for their feelings.
- Seeking reassurance: An ESFP might become clingy or desperately seek approval from others to rebuild their bruised self-esteem.

The key for ESFPs is to acknowledge their vulnerability and stop equating it with weakness. Criticism doesn't mean they are unlovable, and rejection doesn't diminish their worth. It's important for them to find ways to process their emotions healthily, even when it feels uncomfortable.

ESFPs need understanding and patient loved ones who accept their sensitivity. They need space to process their feelings without being judged or made to feel as if they are overreacting. A simple acknowledgment like, "I can see that hurt you," can go a long way in helping them feel less alone.

Key Takeaways from this Section:

- ESFPs are more sensitive than others might realize, and they are heavily impacted by criticism and rejection.
- Their natural inclination is to hide this sensitivity, disguising hurt with humor or withdrawal.
- ESFPs need to learn to accept their vulnerability and develop healthy coping mechanisms.
- They benefit from friends and partners who offer support and understanding without judgment.

The Fear of Being Truly Seen: Intimacy Issues

The ESFP's bright facade can be an effective shield against the world, but it also becomes a barrier to deeper intimacy. When they perpetually play the role of the fun, carefree entertainer, it creates a distance between their true selves and those they care about. The fear of truly being seen is a prevalent challenge for many ESFPs.

This fear has a few main branches:

- Fear of Rejection: If they expose their flaws, imperfections, and deepest insecurities, they worry they won't be loved or accepted.
- Fear of Burdening Others: They don't want their negative emotions to dampen anyone else's spirit.
- Fear of Losing Control: Vulnerability involves handing over some emotional power to another, which can be terrifying for someone used to holding the reigns.

This fear can sabotage relationships, especially romantic ones. The ESFP might pull away at the very moment things feel like they're getting "too serious." They might struggle to communicate their true needs and feelings, or resort to self-sabotaging behaviors to push people away before they get too close.

The irony is that ESFPs deeply crave genuine connection. They yearn for a relationship where they can let down their guard completely and be loved for who they truly are, not just the shiny, happy version of themselves. Achieving authentic intimacy requires a conscious effort to break the pattern of emotional armoring.

This begins with self-awareness:

- Acknowledging the Fear: Simply being aware of their tendency to hide emotionally is a huge step towards change.
- Unpacking the Past: Often, this fear arises from past experiences of rejection or feeling like a burden.
- Finding Safe People: ESFPs need to identify loved ones who are patient, understanding, and offer unconditional support.

Intimacy requires courage. For the ESFP, this means gradually lowering their defenses and allowing carefully chosen people to see their vulnerability. It's about trusting that the right people will love them even more for their imperfections and struggles.

Key Takeaways from this Section:

- ESFPs fear true intimacy because it requires exposing their vulnerabilities.
- This fear can stem from the fear of rejection, burdening others, and losing control.
- ESFPs crave intimate connections but may sabotage their efforts through withdrawal or pushing people away.
- Developing intimacy requires identifying the root of this fear and finding emotionally supportive loved ones.

Building deep intimacy is an ongoing process for an ESFP, but it's a journey that ultimately leads to far more fulfilling relationships and greater self-acceptance.

FEAR OF MISSING OUT (FOMO)

Chasing the Next Best Thing: The ESFP's Restlessness

There's an internal buzz that hums inside many ESFPs, a restless energy that compels them to keep moving, to keep seeking, and to always look for the next thrilling experience. They thrive on the excitement of the unknown, and the prospect of missing out on something amazing fills them with an uneasy sense of dissatisfaction. This is FOMO (the Fear of Missing Out) writ large.

The ESFP's dominant Extroverted Sensing function makes them hyper-aware of all the possibilities that life has to offer. Their minds are constantly scanning their environment, picking up on social cues, new opportunities, and invitations to adventure. There's a palpable fear that while they're busy doing one thing, they might be missing out on something even better somewhere else.

This restlessness can cause several problems:

- Decision Paralysis: The sheer abundance of choices becomes overwhelming, leading to chronic indecisiveness.
- Spread Too Thin: The ESFP might impulsively say "yes" to too many things, overcommitting themselves and eventually leading to burnout.
- Perpetually Dissatisfied: They often compare their experiences, friendships, or possessions to others', feeling like they never quite measure up.
- Missing Out on Depth: Jumping from one experience to another makes it difficult to form deeper bonds or engage with anything on a truly profound level

Social media often amplifies the ESFP's sense of FOMO. The curated highlights of other people's lives can create a false sense of urgency and inadequacy. It's easy for them to fall into the trap of believing everyone else is having more fun, traveling to more exotic places, or achieving more impressive goals.

The key for ESFPs is to learn that the grass isn't always greener on the other side. Developing contentment requires a conscious effort to shift their focus away from what they lack and towards cultivating gratitude for the present moment.

Key Takeaways from this Section:

- ESFPs are highly prone to FOMO due to their love of novelty and their focus on external possibilities.
- This restlessness can cause decision paralysis, overcommitment, and a sense of perpetual dissatisfaction.
- Social media can exacerbate FOMO, creating unrealistic expectations for their own lives.
- Learning to appreciate the present moment is crucial for overcoming FOMO.

The Burden of Choice: Decision-Making Struggles

The ESFP's world teems with possibilities, and with that comes the heavy burden of choice. While spontaneity and adaptability are ESFP strengths, the sheer number of options they constantly encounter can leave them feeling paralyzed with indecision.

Making commitments can be exceptionally difficult. ESFPs worry that every choice cuts off other potential paths, other experiences they might miss out on. It's a paradox: the desire to live life to the fullest makes them reluctant to choose anything that might feel limiting.

This struggle manifests in different ways:

- Procrastination: ESFPs may intentionally delay decisions, believing that a better option will appear or the situation will resolve itself.
- Second-Guessing Themselves: Even after making a choice, they might be plagued with doubts, fearing they've made the wrong decision.

- Avoiding Important Choices: They might find ways to avoid major life decisions about careers, relationships, or where to live, opting for a state of comfortable limbo.
- Seeking Reassurance: ESFPs might constantly consult with others, needing validation of their decisions to avoid taking full responsibility.

The root of this struggle is often a fear of making a mistake or missing out on a better future. Their focus tends to be on what they're giving up, rather than what they're gaining. This can stifle their personal growth and prevent them from moving forward in life.

To overcome this, ESFPs need to:

- Reframe Their Perspective: Instead of seeing decisions as limitations, try viewing them as committing to what excites them right now.
- Trust Their Instincts: ESFPs have strong intuition when it comes to what feels right in the present. It's helpful to tune back into that.
- Let Go of Perfectionism: Accept that there's no perfect choice, and trust their ability to adapt to whatever path they take.
- Start Small: Practice making minor, low-stakes decisions helps build their decision-making muscle and boost their confidence.

While decisions can be stressful for an ESFP, it's important to remember that choice is a privilege, and the act of making a choice, even an imperfect one, is a form of exercising their freedom and steering the course of their own lives.

Key Takeaways from this Section:

- ESFPs can be paralyzed by decision-making, fearing limits on their freedom and potential experiences.
- This indecision can lead to procrastination, second-guessing, and avoiding important life choices.

- To overcome this, ESFPs need to reframe decisions as positive and learn to trust their instincts.

Learning to make choices from a place of confidence rather than fear will free the ESFP to embrace the potential that lies on whichever path they choose.

THE STRUGGLE FOR FOCUS

Easily Distracted: Battling Shiny Object Syndrome

The ESFP mind is a kaleidoscope of vibrant possibilities. They have an incredible ability to pick up on details and potential connections, their senses constantly bombarded with exciting new stimuli. Unfortunately, this brilliance comes with a downside: ESFPs are notoriously prone to distraction. Their focus can flit from one thing to the next with hummingbird-like speed, making it difficult to sustain concentration on a single task.

This difficulty in focusing often gets referred to as "Shiny Object Syndrome." ESFPs are easily lured by anything novel, shiny, or simply more interesting than the task at hand. A text message notification, an interesting conversation overheard across the room, or even a random thought that pops into their heads can completely derail their train of thought.

This lack of focus can cause a myriad of problems:

- Procrastination Perfect Trap: ESFPs get excited about starting projects but soon lose interest when their focus wanes. Procrastination becomes their default mode.
- Difficulty Finishing What They Start: They may have several half-finished projects due to their tendency to bounce between tasks or ideas.
- Missing Important Details: Their focus scattering between multiple things can lead to careless errors or missing crucial information.
- Time Management Troubles: Losing track of time is a common issue, making it difficult for ESFPs to stick to schedules or meet deadlines.

It's important to understand that the ESFP isn't lazy or incapable of focusing; their brains simply work differently. The world they experience is so rich and multi-faceted that it becomes easy to lose sight of the less captivating task in front of them. This can be extremely frustrating for them, as they often have the desire and ambition to accomplish great things if only they could harness their energy more effectively.

This tendency to find focus difficult can be especially challenging in traditional school or work environments that demand long periods of sustained concentration on less-than-thrilling tasks. ESFPs may feel discouraged and develop a negative self-image of being incapable or unreliable, when the issue is more about their environment not being a natural fit for their cognitive style.

Key Takeaways from this Section:

- ESFPs have active minds that constantly scan their environment, easily picking up on interesting details or possibilities.
- This mental agility makes them prone to distraction and "Shiny Object Syndrome".
- Distractibility leads to problems with procrastination, task completion, and time management.
- ESFPs are not lazy, they simply have brains that are wired for a different type of stimulation.

Commitment and Follow-Through: A Work in Progress

While focus and discipline might not be their strongest suits, ESFPs are adaptable and possess a remarkable ability to learn and grow. Committing to developing better focus might be a work in progress, but it's a journey that brings considerable rewards. With some self-awareness, strategy, and a little trial and error, ESFPs can learn to channel their natural energy towards greater productivity and follow-through.

Here's a toolkit for ESFPs to develop better focus:

- Structure with Flexibility: ESFPs loathe rigid routines, so creating structure that allows for spontaneity is key. Break large tasks into smaller, manageable chunks, and schedule short bursts of focused work with built-in breaks for mental refreshers.

- Minimize Distractions: ESFPs need distraction-free environments to work effectively. Find a quiet space, turn off phone notifications, and resist the urge to multitask.
- Gamify the Mundane: Make boring tasks more appealing by adding an element of competition, reward, or novelty. Set timers, challenge yourself to beat previous records, or use colorful sticky notes to visually track progress.
- Leverage Passion: ESFPs will naturally focus on what excites them. Find ways to connect less-interesting tasks to a bigger goal or find the aspect that sparks your curiosity.
- The Accountability Buddy: Find someone understanding to check in with your progress, offering gentle nudges or celebrating your victories.
- Prioritize Rest and Play: ESFPs drain quickly when they don't have sufficient time to unwind, leading to more scattered thinking. Schedule downtime and engage in activities they truly enjoy.

It's crucial for ESFPs to acknowledge that focus is a skill, not a personality flaw. They need to develop a sense of self-compassion and patience with themselves. It also means celebrating small wins and adjusting strategies as needed – what works one day might not work the next.

The truth is, some ESFPs will always thrive in environments that offer variety, spontaneity, and high levels of social interaction. They might be better suited to careers that align with these strengths rather than trying to force themselves into a traditional 9-to-5 box that never quite fits.

Key Takeaways from this Section:

- ESFPs can improve their focus with strategies tailored towards their unique cognitive style.
- Creating a flexible structure, minimizing distractions, and

gamifying tasks can help.
- Connecting tasks to their passions and utilizing accountability systems offer greater support.
- Self-compassion and celebrating small wins are crucial throughout this learning process.
- For some ESFPs, finding careers aligned with their strengths might be the ultimate key to avoiding constant battles with focus.

With a playful but determined approach, ESFPs can gradually build their focus muscles, creating a life where their brilliant ideas get the chance to shine through to completion.

UNLOCKING INTROSPECTION

Finding Quiet Moments: The Importance of Reflection

The world of the ESFP is vibrantly external. They are fueled by interaction, thrive on sensory input, and often use activity and social connection as a means of processing the world around them. However, to find true balance and unlock their full potential, ESFPs need to cultivate the often-overlooked art of introspection.

Think of the ESFP mind as a stunning fireworks display – a brilliant explosion of light and color. Yet, even the most dazzling show needs moments of darkness in between for the full beauty to be appreciated. Introspection for the ESFP is that period of darkness, a time to pause, reflect, and integrate their experiences.

Why does introspection matter for ESFPs? Here's what it offers:

- Enhanced Self-awareness: Quiet reflection allows ESFPs to identify patterns in their behavior, understand their emotions, and develop greater clarity about their values and goals.
- Improved Decision-Making: Taking time to think deeper helps ESFPs connect decisions to their internal compass rather than being swayed solely by external factors.
- Emotional Regulation: Introspection helps them process difficult emotions, leading to healthier coping mechanisms and preventing emotional outbursts.
- Greater Empathy: By turning that powerful observation inward, they develop a deeper understanding of themselves, which fosters greater empathy and connection with others.

While introspection seems counterintuitive to the ESFP's nature, it's important to remember they have a rich inner world, even if they don't access it as often. Their introverted feeling, while less dominant, is a wellspring of personal values and sensitivities waiting to be explored.

The challenge is making introspection appealing and sustainable for the ESFP. Rigid, forced meditation likely won't work and could even lead to frustration.

Key Takeaways from this Section:

- Introspection offers ESFPs a counterbalance to their external focus, contributing to better self-understanding and overall well-being.
- Quiet reflection enhances decision-making, emotional regulation, and empathy.
- ESFPs have an inner world to explore, but they might need to approach introspection in a way that feels natural and engaging to them.

Facing Inner Demons: Dealing with Unresolved Issues

ESFPs are often masters of living in the moment, pushing away uncomfortable emotions in favor of seeking immediate joy and distraction. While this serves them well in the short term, it can lead to unresolved issues festering beneath the surface. Introspection is the key to pulling back the curtain and facing those shadows.

Think of unresolved issues as emotional baggage that the ESFP has been hastily shoving into closets and under the bed of their psyche. The longer it remains out-of-sight, the more it grows, creating invisible blockages and hindering their true growth.

Examples of unresolved issues ESFPs might grapple with:

- Past Hurts and Betrayals: Holding onto resentment or pain from experiences where they felt deeply wounded or let down.
- Unprocessed Anxieties: Unacknowledged worries about failure, rejection, or not being "enough" that manifest in other ways.

- Suppressed Anger: Difficulty expressing anger constructively, leading to it either being bottled up or exploding at inappropriate moments.
- Lingering Grief: Avoiding dealing with the pain of loss, whether it's from a relationship breakup, death of someone close, or the loss of a dream.

Introspection provides a safe space for ESFPs to acknowledge these unresolved issues. It can be scary, as facing them involves confronting uncomfortable feelings they've expertly avoided. However, it's the first step to healing and breaking free from the negative ways these buried issues may be influencing their behavior.

Here's how ESFPs can begin tackling unresolved issues:

- Identify Triggers: Start by noticing patterns. When do you feel disproportionately angry, hurt, or afraid? These moments may point to a deeper, unresolved wound.
- Journaling: Expressing emotions through writing can be a powerful way to process without the need to share or explain.
- Talking It Out: Find a trusted friend or a therapist who is non-judgmental and offers the space to feel their emotions fully.
- Embracing Vulnerability: Allow yourself to cry, grieve, or express anger in a healthy way. These feelings aren't weaknesses but signs of processing.

The journey of addressing unresolved issues won't happen overnight for an ESFP. Their inclination is to find a quick fix and move on. Yet, facing these deeper layers of themselves offers profound rewards. It frees up energy previously spent on avoidance, allows them to build more authentic relationships, and helps them develop emotional resilience they need for a truly fulfilling life.

Key Takeaways from this Section:

- ESFPs may carry unresolved emotional baggage that hampers their growth and well-being.
- Introspection allows them to identify and address past hurts, anxieties, anger, and grief.
- Seeking support through journaling, talking to a trusted person, or therapy can help them process these emotions.
- Though difficult, facing unresolved issues leads to greater self-awareness, healthier relationships, and emotional resilience.

THE PARADOX OF PLANNING

Living Spontaneously: When Structure Feels Stifling

If you tell an ESFP they need to create a detailed 5-year plan, they'll likely either laugh in your face or start to feel a creeping sense of panic. ESFPs are guided by a love for spontaneity, embracing the unpredictable flow of life with remarkable adaptability. Structure, long-term plans, and rigid routines can feel suffocating, like they're being robbed of the joy of the unknown.

This aversion to planning originates from a few key places:

- Fear of Limits: ESFPs fear that committing to a plan will close off other possibilities and unforeseen opportunities.
- Desire for Freedom: They deeply value their sense of autonomy and freedom to make choices in the moment, based on their gut feeling.
- Restlessness: The idea of staying on the same path for a prolonged period can feel incredibly boring, leading to a fear of stagnation.
- Craving Constant Stimulation: ESFPs crave the excitement of novelty; structured plans often involve delayed gratification which can feel frustrating.

The ESFP's present-oriented focus is both a strength and a challenge. Their ability to embrace the moment allows them to find joy in simple things and adapt quickly to unexpected changes. However, this constant focus on the "now" can lead to impulsivity, difficulty setting long-term goals, and a chaotic life where commitments often fall by the wayside.

ESFPs often operate under the belief that things will work themselves out. This optimistic outlook can be a wonderful asset, but it can also lead to a lack of preparation and a tendency to wing it rather than think ahead about potential consequences.

Finding a healthy middle ground is essential. ESFPs need to learn the importance of having some structure in their lives without losing their essence. It's about striking a balance between spontaneity and just enough planning to avoid constant self-created chaos.

Key Takeaways from this Section:

- ESFPs have a natural aversion to long-term planning and rigid schedules.
- Their desire for freedom, spontaneity, and flexibility underlies this resistance.
- Their focus on the present-moment, while beautiful, can lead to impulsivity and difficulty achieving long-term goals.
- ESFPs thrive in a balance between spontaneity and a basic level of necessary structure.

The Need for (Flexible) Plans: Finding a Balance

Let's be clear: ESFPs will never be the type who meticulously plans out every day or maps out their life a decade in advance. However, a touch of strategic planning can go a long way in maximizing their potential and minimizing the chaos that often comes with a completely "winging it" attitude.

Here's how ESFPs can start incorporating flexible planning:

- Focus on Big Picture Goals: What do you want your life to look like in broad strokes? What experiences matter to you? This helps provide a sense of direction without rigid details.
- Embrace Short-Term Planning: Break down larger goals into smaller, achievable steps with flexible timelines. Weekly or even daily to-do lists can be helpful if they feel attainable.
- Prioritize, Don't Schedule: Instead of trying to schedule every hour, focus on prioritizing what's important and then fitting those into your day where they naturally work.
- The Loose Itinerary: Whether it's an upcoming trip or even a weekend, have a general outline but leave plenty of room for

unplanned, spontaneous adventures along the way.

- Build in Time for the Unexpected: Recognizing their love for the unplanned, ESFPs can schedule buffer zones into their week, ensuring time for last-minute invitations or a sudden change of plans.
- Delegate and Outsource: If certain tasks feel suffocating, figure out if you can delegate them to someone else to free up time for the things you truly enjoy.

Benefits of flexible planning for ESFPs:

- Reduced Stress: Having some structure lowers anxiety and feelings of life being out of control.
- Greater Achievement: Planning helps create forward movement towards their desired goals.
- More Free Time: Counterintuitively, planning saves time by avoiding last-minute scrambles or procrastination cycles.
- Avoiding Burnout: ESFPs tend to run full speed and then crash. Planning helps pace their energy for better long-term sustainability.

It's important for ESFPs to approach planning with a sense of playfulness and experimentation. Finding systems that work for them is key. This might mean brightly colored sticky notes, mobile apps, or simply a notebook dedicated to their ever-evolving master plan.

The goal isn't to become a different personality type. The goal is to harness the ESFP's natural brilliance within a structure that allows them to create a life that is both joyfully spontaneous and intentionally fulfilling.

Key Takeaways from this Section:

- ESFPs benefit from a flexible planning approach that prioritizes their values and leaves room for spontaneity.
- Focusing on big-picture goals, short-term steps, and loose outlines can provide direction without feeling restrictive.
- Planning can actually increase freedom and reduce stress by

allowing ESFPs to achieve their goals and avoid overwhelm.
- Finding enjoyable and adaptable planning tools supports long-term success.

SEEKING DEEPER MEANING

Beyond Superficial Pleasures: Finding Life Purpose

ESFPs are often seen as the quintessential pleasure-seekers, drawn to the tantalizing tastes, vibrant sights, and exhilarating experiences the world offers. However, underneath the surface lies a yearning for something more, a desire to find deeper meaning and purpose in life.

The ESFP's innate curiosity can sometimes lead them down a rabbit hole of flitting from one interest to the next, chasing short bursts of excitement. While these experiences bring them joy, that feeling can be fleeting. There's often a nagging sense that they haven't yet found their true calling, leaving them feeling unfulfilled and frustrated that their boundless energy doesn't have a greater focus.

Their search for deeper meaning could manifest in a few ways:

- Existential Questions: ESFPs may find themselves pondering the bigger questions of life – Why am I here? What's the point of it all?
- Craving Connection to Something Larger: They may feel a desire to be part of a cause greater than themselves or to make a tangible difference in the world.
- Questioning the Status Quo: ESFPs, with their natural inclination to seek new possibilities, might start to question societal norms and explore alternative ways of living.
- Spiritual Exploration: They might embark on a spiritual journey, seeking a stronger sense of connectedness to the universe or a belief system that aligns with their values.

The path to discovering meaning and purpose is deeply individual, but here are some guiding questions that can help an ESFP start their journey:

- When do you feel most alive? What activities engage your heart, excite your mind, and leave you feeling a sense of satisfaction long after the moment passes?
- What breaks your heart? Identifying the injustices or problems in the world that stir strong emotions within you can be a signpost towards areas where you can make a difference.
- What legacy do you want to leave behind? If you look far into the future, what impact do you hope to have had on the lives of others or on the world around you?

Finding their purpose won't be an overnight revelation for an ESFP. It's a process of exploration, trial and error, and learning what truly resonates with their soul. This journey might involve trying new things, pursuing passions outside of their usual comfort zone, and pushing themselves to delve deeper into experiences that initially seem solely focused on surface-level joy.

Key Takeaways from this Section:

- ESFPs, despite their reputation for enjoying the moment, often have a deeply rooted desire to find meaning and purpose in life.
- They may find themselves questioning existence, seeking a cause greater than themselves, or exploring spiritual beliefs.
- Discovering their purpose involves identifying their passions, addressing causes that ignite their empathy, and envisioning the legacy they want to leave.
- This journey is a process of self-discovery that involves embracing new experiences, introspection, and a willingness to explore beyond the surface.

The ESFP's Spiritual Journey: Finding Connection to Something Larger

ESFPs are not conventionally known for their spiritual side. Their focus on the tangible world and immediate experiences might seem at odds with the esoteric realm of spirituality. However, their open-mindedness, deep empathy, and desire to live life to the fullest can lead them down a unique and impactful spiritual path.

The ESFP's form of spirituality is less about dogma and more about direct experience. Here's where their strengths shine:

- Connection to Nature: ESFPs often feel a profound sense of awe when immersed in the beauty of the natural world. Hiking, camping, or simply watching a sunset can spark feelings of deep interconnectedness and wonder.
- The Power of Present-Moment Awareness: While unintentional, the ESFP's ability to be fully absorbed in the present aligns beautifully with the core of many mindfulness and spiritual practices.
- Finding Transcendence through Joy: ESFPs understand how music, art, dance, or other forms of creative expression can transport them to an elevated state of consciousness.
- Service to Others: Their powerful empathy often fuels a desire to contribute positively to the world, a key tenet of many spiritual traditions.

A few ways spirituality may manifest in an ESFP's life:

- Exploration of Different Beliefs: An ESFP may be curious about different religions and philosophies, sampling from various traditions without rigid adherence to any one doctrine.
- A Focus on Personal Growth: Spirituality may be viewed as a path to becoming a better, more loving, and more compassionate person.
- Mindfulness and Meditation: While traditional meditation might be a struggle, ESFPs can find their own form of mindfulness through activities that fully engage their senses and quiet the mental chatter.
- Energy Work & Healing: Given their awareness of subtle dynamics, they may be drawn to energy work like Reiki, or healing modalities focused on the mind-body connection.

It's important to note that not all ESFPs will feel a pull towards spirituality. For those that do, the key is finding what feels authentic and meaningful to them. Their spiritual journey will likely be unconventional, experiential, and deeply personal.

Here's the beauty in the ESFP's approach: they infuse spirituality into life itself. They find the sacred in the simple moments of joy, in the vibrant connections with others, and in the awe-inspiring power of the present. It's a testament to the fact that a deep spiritual life can take on many forms, and the ESFP's path is uniquely beautiful.

Key Takeaways from this Section:

- ESFPs can find profound spiritual connection through experiences in nature, present-moment awareness, creativity, and service to others.
- Their spirituality may be less focused on strict doctrine and more about direct experience and connection to something larger than themselves.
- ESFPs often explore different spiritual paths, finding elements that resonate deeply on a personal level.
- The ESFP's spiritual expression is infused into everyday life, finding the sacred in the simple and joyful.

CRAVING AUTHENTICITY

Breaking Free from Expectations: Being the Real You

There's a hidden cost to being the life of the party. ESFPs often feel pressure, whether consciously or subconsciously, to uphold their persona of the carefree, vivacious entertainer. While they undoubtedly love bringing joy to those around them, the constant performance can become draining if it means always hiding their true selves.

ESFPs long for authenticity. They desire to be seen, understood, and loved for who they genuinely are – flaws, vulnerabilities, weird quirks, and all. But fear of judgment, rejection, or appearing weak can hold them back from letting their guard down fully.

Societal expectations weigh heavily on ESFPs. Here's where they might feel stifled:

- "Always Be Positive" Pressure: ESFPs are often told to "look on the bright side" or "cheer up" when they're feeling down, which can lead to them suppressing their true emotions.
- Perpetual Performer Role: There's an expectation for ESFPs to be "on" all the time, entertaining and making others feel good, even when they need a break.
- Image Over Substance: Focus on appearances, popularity, and external validation can lead ESFPs to prioritizing what others think over their own internal compass.
- "Perfect Friend" Trap: Their loyal and empathetic nature can make it difficult to set boundaries in friendships, leading to them suppressing their own needs to please others.

The path to authenticity for an ESFP begins with self-awareness. They need to become attuned to the subtle ways they adjust their behavior to fit other people's expectations. This might involve some uncomfortable introspection:

- Identifying Triggers: What situations make you feel the need to put on a facade? What types of people are you most likely to perform for?
- Recognizing the Mask: Observe how you present yourself differently around different groups or individuals.
- Acknowledging Hidden Emotions: What feelings do you suppress to keep up the image of being the fun-loving, carefree one?

Breaking free from expectations is an ongoing process. It's about giving yourself permission to be a multi-faceted human being – the joyful, sparkling social butterfly AND the person who sometimes needs quiet time, feels insecure, or experiences sadness.

Key Takeaways from this Section:

- ESFPs strongly desire to be genuinely understood and loved for their full selves, not just their social persona.
- Societal pressure to be constantly positive and entertaining can lead to suppression of true emotions.
- ESFPs need to become aware of how they change their behavior to fit what others expect.
- The journey to authenticity involves allowing themselves to experience and express the full range of human emotions.

When Image is Everything: Losing Yourself in the Performance

For ESFPs, image can be a double-edged sword. On one hand, their natural charisma and ability to connect with others are genuine strengths. On the other hand, the focus on how they're perceived, fueled by a deep desire to be loved and accepted, can lead them astray. When image becomes all-consuming, they risk losing touch with their authentic selves.

There's immense pressure for ESFPs to curate an image of the perfect life – the fun-loving friend, the effortlessly stylish individual, the one with an exciting social calendar. When their self-worth becomes overly attached to these external factors, it creates a dangerous cycle:

- Superficial Validation: They may seek validation through social media likes, compliments on their appearance, or the envy of others.
- People Pleasing in Overdrive: ESFPs may become obsessed with trying themselves into who they think others want them to be, suppressing their own desires in the process.
- Materialism & Overspending: The focus on image can lead to overspending on clothes, experiences, or other status symbols to impress others or feel good about themselves.
- Neglecting the Inner World: Obsessing over external appearances distracts from internal growth, leaving the ESFP feeling empty despite their seemingly fabulous life.

The tragedy of losing oneself in the performance is that the very thing ESFPs crave – genuine connection – becomes impossible. They end up surrounded by people who love a curated version of them, not the real person beneath the façade.

The path to reclaiming authenticity involves a shift in focus:

- Question Your Motives: Before posting that selfie or buying that new outfit, ask yourself, "Am I doing this for me or to impress others?"
- Prioritize Meaningful Connections: Seek out people who love you for who you are on the inside, who accept your flaws and celebrate your quirks
- Celebrate Your Imperfections: Embracing "messiness" is incredibly liberating. Share your struggles, show your goofy side, laugh at your mistakes.
- Practice Self-Compassion: Be kind to yourself as you break free from image obsession. There is no shame in having been caught up in the performance; there is only power in choosing to be true to yourself.

ESFPs are radiant beings with the ability to bring joy and genuine connection to the world. When they shed the weight of image obsession, their natural sparkle shines even brighter.

Key Takeaways from this Section:

- ESFPs can become overly focused on curating an image, seeking external validation to fuel their self-worth.
- Prioritizing image leads to superficial connections, neglect of their inner development, and can even impact their spending habits.
- Reclaiming authenticity involves questioning motives, seeking meaningful relationships, and embracing their perfectly imperfect selves.
- True freedom for an ESFP lies in being loved for who they genuinely are and shining brightly from the inside out.

THE GIFT OF EMPATHY

The ESFP's Superpower: Connecting Deeply with Others

ESFPs, often hailed as "The Performers," are renowned for their infectious enthusiasm, social charisma, and ability to light up any room. But beneath the dazzling exterior lies a powerful and often underestimated strength: a deep wellspring of empathy. The ESFP's gift of empathy allows them to form extraordinary connections, offer unwavering support, and act as an emotional beacon for those around them.

Understanding ESFP Empathy

While ESFPs are known for their focus on the external world (Extroverted Sensing), they possess a potent secondary function: Introverted Feeling. This means that in addition to being highly attuned to the sensory details of their environment, they also place significant value on the emotional atmosphere and the internal experiences of others. They are like emotional radars, sensing subtle shifts in mood, picking up on unspoken sadness, and instinctively knowing when someone needs their support.

Here's how the ESFP's empathy manifests itself:

- Emotional Mirroring: ESFPs have an uncanny ability to mirror the emotions of those around them. If you feel excited, they feel your excitement. If you're hurting, their hearts ache with yours. This makes people feel deeply seen and understood.
- Walking in Your Shoes: They don't just observe your emotions, they try to step into your shoes and understand the world through your eyes. This intuitive empathy enables them to offer support that is truly relevant and helpful.
- The Energy Shifters: ESFPs know how to change the emotional tone of a situation. With their warmth and

humor, they can uplift a downcast friend, ease tension in a conflict, or simply bring a ray of sunshine into someone's day.

- Emotional Cheerleaders: When you're feeling insecure or doubtful, an ESFP will be your biggest cheerleader. They believe in you wholeheartedly and express their confidence with such enthusiasm that you can't help but feel bolstered.

Beyond the Smile: The Importance of Acknowledging ESFP Empathy

It's easy to mistake the ESFP's focus on creating a positive atmosphere as a sign of shallowness when the opposite is often true. Their desire to make others feel good stems from a deep-seated empathy and a genuine wish to uplift those around them. It's important to recognize that behind their smiles and lighthearted energy often lies a caring heart that feels deeply for others.

When Empathy Becomes a Burden

The ESFP's powerful empathy is a gift, but it can also be a heavy burden. Here's where they might struggle:

- Absorbing Others' Emotions: ESFPs can easily become overwhelmed by the negativity around them, absorbing the pain and stress of others as if it were their own.
- Difficulty Setting Boundaries: Their desire to help can lead to them bending over backward for others, neglecting their own needs in the process.
- Personalizing Others' Pain: ESFPs may take it personally when they can't fix someone's problems or make them feel better, leading to feelings of inadequacy or self-blame.
- Emotional Burnout: Without healthy boundaries and self-care, ESFPs can reach a point of emotional exhaustion, feeling drained and depleted.

Tips for ESFPs to Manage Their Gift of Empathy

To ensure their empathy remains a source of strength, ESFPs need to learn to care for their own emotional well-being. Here's how:

- Practice Self-Awareness: Pay attention to how the emotions of others are impacting you. Learn to recognize the signs when you're becoming overwhelmed.
- Set Boundaries: It's okay to say "no" or to take some time for yourself to recharge. Helping others doesn't mean sacrificing your own needs.
- Practice Self-Care: Engage in activities that nurture your soul, whether it's spending time in nature, exercising, listening to good music, or simply taking time to relax.
- Find Healthy Outlets: Express your own emotions through journaling, talking to a trusted friend, or engaging in creative activities.
- Develop Mindfulness: Practicing mindfulness can help you stay present with your own emotions rather than becoming completely entangled in those of others.

It's important to note that learning to manage their empathy in healthy ways doesn't mean ESFPs should shut themselves off from the feelings of others. Their gift is an integral part of who they are. However, finding balance is key to harnessing the power of their empathy for both themselves and those they care about.

The Challenge of Boundaries: When Caring Hurts

The ESFP's innate desire to help and their boundless empathy can sometimes lead to blurred boundaries in their relationships. Their big hearts and focus on making others happy can make it difficult for them to differentiate where their emotional responsibility ends and another person's begins.

Here's how this plays out in different types of relationships:

- Friends in Need: When a friend is going through a rough patch, the ESFP's instinct is to rush to their side and try to fix the situation. They may offer advice, become emotionally invested in their friend's problems, or take on practical tasks to ease the burden. While well-intentioned, this can create an unhealthy dynamic where the friend relies too heavily on the ESFP or where the ESFP feels responsible for their friend's happiness.

- Romantic Entanglements: ESFPs often fall hard and fast in love. When swept up in a new romance, their focus on their partner can overshadow their focus on themselves. They might lose themselves in trying to anticipate their partner's needs, make the relationship perfect, or avoid potential conflict with an overly accommodating stance.

- Family Dynamics: ESFPs often feel a deep sense of responsibility within their families, particularly towards siblings or older relatives. They may act as peacemakers, shoulder the burdens of others, or sacrifice their own needs to create harmony.

Why Setting Healthy Boundaries is Essential for ESFPs

- Preventing Codependency: When boundaries are weak, ESFPs can find themselves in codependent relationships where they take on an unhealthy amount of responsibility for others' well-being.

- Avoiding Resentment: Overextending themselves for others can create a buildup of unspoken resentment that can ultimately damage their relationships.

- Preserving Self-Worth: Their sense of worth can become deeply tied to the well-being of others, leaving them vulnerable to emotional devastation if someone they care for is hurting.

- Protecting Their Own Energy: Without boundaries, the ESFP's vibrant energy reserves can become depleted, impacting their own happiness and ability to show up as their best selves.

Strategies for Setting Healthy Boundaries

This can be incredibly challenging for ESFPs - fear of letting people down or causing conflict is ever-present. Here's how to gently start:

- Learn to Say "No": Practice small acts of refusal. It could be declining an invitation, saying no to a favor, or voicing disagreement.
- Offer Alternative Support: Instead of diving in to solve someone's problem, suggest other resources or simply offer a listening ear.
- "I need some space": Be ok with taking time for yourself, whether it's a few minutes alone or a weekend to recharge.
- State Your Needs: Practice clearly communicating what you do and don't need from others.
- Seek Emotional Support: ESFPs need safe people who THEY can lean on during tough times so they don't become everyone else's support system.

Setting boundaries is a skill built over time. ESFPs may feel initial guilt or worry about hurting others' feelings. It's important for them to understand that establishing healthy boundaries is actually an act of self-love and ultimately creates stronger, more authentic relationships with those they care about.

The Power of Balanced Empathy

The ESFP's gift of empathy is a precious asset to the world. It's a source of joy, support, and deep connection for those lucky enough to have an ESFP in their lives. When ESFPs manage their empathy with strong boundaries and healthy self-care, they avoid burnout and can use their remarkable ability to understand and uplift others in a way that is both sustainable and incredibly powerful.

EMOTIONAL INTELLIGENCE

Understanding Your Feelings: Tuning into Your Inner World

ESFPs are often so attuned to the emotions of those around them that they can lose touch with their own internal landscape. They are masters at creating positive and joyful experiences in their outer world, but sometimes this focus on the external can lead to a neglect of their own emotional well-being.

Developing a greater level of emotional intelligence is key for ESFPs. Emotional intelligence involves the ability to understand, manage, and express their own emotions in healthy ways and to skillfully navigate the complexities of interpersonal relationships. While their natural empathy gives them a head start, there's always room for growth.

Here's where ESFPs might struggle with emotions:

- The Emotional Bottleneck: ESFPs often push aside negative emotions in favor of seeking immediate joy. While this works in the short term, unprocessed emotions don't disappear. They fester and can manifest as angry outbursts, unexplained anxiety, or even physical health issues.
- Difficulty with Vulnerability: Sharing their deepest fears, insecurities, or sadness doesn't come naturally. There's a fear of being judged, rejected, or appearing weak by expressing anything other than positivity.
- "I'm Fine" Syndrome: ESFPs may fall into the habit of automatically saying "I'm fine" even when they're not. This stems from a desire to avoid burdening others and a worry of disrupting the positive energy they strive to create.
- Misreading Their Own Needs: Their focus on making others happy can cause them to neglect their own emotional needs until they reach a point of breaking.

Why Developing Emotional Intelligence Matters for ESFPs

Strong emotional intelligence allows ESFPs to:

- Build Deeper Relationships: Being able to express their true emotions and openly discuss difficult topics builds stronger, more authentic connections.
- Improve Self-Awareness: Understanding their own emotional patterns helps them identify triggers and develop healthy coping mechanisms.
- Manage Stress & Prevent Burnout: Learning to process difficult emotions before they become overwhelming is crucial for maintaining mental and emotional well-being.
- Enhance Their Empathy: By developing a deeper understanding of their own emotional world, their ability to connect with and support others becomes even stronger.
- Make Better Decisions: When they are in tune with their own emotions, they are better equipped to make decisions that are aligned with their true values and long-term happiness.

Starting the Journey: Tools for an ESFP

ESFPs won't transform into masters of emotional introspection overnight. But developing greater emotional intelligence begins with these steps:

- Emotional Vocabulary: Expand your vocabulary for describing your inner world. Go beyond basic feelings like "happy" or "mad" and explore the nuances of your emotional experience.
- Notice Body Sensations: Pay attention to how your body reacts in different emotional states. Where do you feel sadness? What does anger feel like physically?
- Journaling: Writing down your feelings without judgment helps you untangle and process them.
- Mindful Moments: Practice pausing a few times a day to simply check in with your emotions. Just observe how you're feeling without trying to fix, change, or dismiss anything.

Developing greater emotional awareness is an ongoing journey for ESFPs. It will likely feel uncomfortable at first, but the rewards in terms of greater well-being and deeper connection with both themselves and others are immensely valuable.

Healthy Expression: Avoiding Emotional Outbursts

ESFPs are known for their warmth, enthusiasm, and infectious energy. Yet, the very intensity of their emotions can sometimes lead to unexpected outbursts. Bottling up their feelings, prioritizing positivity, and a fear of vulnerability create a situation which, over time, can lead to unexpected eruptions of anger, frustration, or overwhelming sadness.

It may seem like these outbursts come out of nowhere, but they are often the result of pent-up emotions that haven't been processed or expressed healthily. This can be confusing and hurtful to those around the ESFP and can even create a sense of internal shame or embarrassment that further complicates their emotional regulation.

Strategies for Healthy Emotional Expression

Learning to express their emotions in healthier ways is a crucial aspect of the ESFP's personal growth. Here are some more helpful strategies:

- Find Safe Outlets: Identify activities that help the ESFP release pent-up emotions. Exercise, dancing, screaming into a pillow, creating art – there's no right or wrong way as long as it's not harming themselves or others.
- The Trusted Confidant: Find someone they trust and feel safe with to confide their vulnerabilities in. Simply expressing their emotions out loud, even if it's messy, can provide incredible relief.
- "I Feel..." Statements: Learn to express emotions calmly and directly using "I feel..." statements. For example, instead of a frustrated outburst, they can say, "I feel overwhelmed and

stressed right now. I need some space."

- Taking a Pause: When they feel emotions escalating, it's incredibly helpful for an ESFP to take a step back before reacting. A short walk, deep breaths, or listening to calming music can help them settle enough to express themselves more effectively.
- Accepting Tears: Crying is a natural release of sadness, frustration, or even overwhelming joy. ESFPs need to give themselves permission to experience this without judgment.

Importantly, developing healthier emotional expression doesn't mean ESFPs have to stop being their upbeat, positive selves. It's about finding a balance. With practice, they can learn to acknowledge and express the full spectrum of their emotions without letting negativity consume them.

The Importance of Self-Compassion

ESFPs tend to be hard on themselves when they have emotional outbursts, as it goes against their self-image of the joyful, easygoing person. Self-compassion is key. They need to understand that these outbursts are often a sign of unprocessed emotions that they're still learning to navigate.

Instead of berating themselves, they need to practice gentle self-talk. Reminding themselves that everyone has occasional moments of emotional overwhelm and that they are allowed to feel the full range of human emotions is helpful. Seeking support from understanding loved ones, or even considering therapy if emotional regulation becomes a significant struggle, can provide the needed encouragement during this process.

Emotional Intelligence as a Path to Authenticity and Deeper Connection

For ESFPs, emotional intelligence isn't about becoming someone different; it's about embracing their wholeness. By learning to recognize, understand, and express their emotions in healthier ways, they become even better equipped to connect with others authentically and build lasting, loving relationships built on both joy and genuine emotional honesty.

TAPPING INTO CREATIVITY

The Artistic ESFP: Finding Expression Through Art

ESFPs are naturally wired for creativity. Their vibrant energy, keen observation skills, and deep appreciation for the beauty of the sensory world equip them with boundless potential for artistic expression. However, their focus on immediate experience and living in the present moment can sometimes lead to their creative talents remaining undiscovered or underdeveloped.

Creativity for the ESFP is not limited to traditional artistic forms. Their creativity manifests in a myriad of ways:

- Problem-solving Virtuosos: ESFPs have an incredible knack for finding innovative and unconventional solutions. They think outside the box, bringing fresh perspectives to challenges.
- Style Gurus: They have a natural flair for fashion, interior design, or creating visually appealing presentations. Their sense of aesthetics adds a unique touch to everything they create.
- Masters of Improvisation: ESFPs are masters of adapting and thinking on their feet. In work or social situations, they can come up with creative solutions in the moment or turn an unexpected snag into an amusing anecdote.
- The Art of Storytelling: They have a gift for bringing stories to life with captivating enthusiasm and a natural sense of humor. Their tales are filled with vivid detail and infectious energy.
- Creating Experiences: ESFPs know how to create memorable experiences for others. Whether it's planning a surprise party, organizing a themed event, or simply transforming an ordinary gathering into something special, they have a knack for bringing fun and excitement into any situation.

Unlocking the ESFP's Creative Potential

Many ESFPs underestimate or are even unaware of their own creative talents. Here's how they can start to tap into their creative flow:

- Embrace Playfulness: Creativity thrives in an atmosphere of joy and experimentation. ESFPs need to give themselves permission to play, doodle, make silly things, or try new things without worrying about the end product.
- Try New Things: Dabbling in different forms of creative expression can spark unexpected interests. Taking a dance class, trying their hand at painting, or joining a writing group can lead to fulfilling discoveries.
- Make Time for Fun: ESFPs often prioritize socializing, chores, or other obligations. Deliberately carve out time in their schedules specifically for creative exploration, no matter how small the time block is.
- Don't Judge the Process: Focus on enjoyment rather than perfection. The ESFP's inner critic can sometimes stifle their creative expression. Remind themselves that the act of creation in itself is valuable, whether or not the outcome is a masterpiece.
- Find Your Tribe: Connecting with other creatives is incredibly inspiring. Seek out workshops, artist groups, or simply friends who enjoy creative hobbies and share the journey with them.

Why Creativity Matters for ESFPs

Developing their creative side offers numerous benefits:

- Emotional Outlet: Creative expression provides a powerful channel for processing emotions, whether consciously or subconsciously.
- Stress Relief & Mental Wellness: Engaging in creative activities can be a joyful escape from worries, promoting relaxation and reducing anxiety.

- Boosting Self-Confidence: Expressing themselves creatively and seeing what they can bring into the world builds a strong sense of self-confidence.
- Source of Purpose & Meaning: Creative pursuits can add a deeper sense of fulfillment and purpose to the ESFP's life.
- Enhancing Relationships: Sharing their creativity with others - whether it's a home-cooked meal, a silly song, or a piece of art - brings them closer to loved ones.

It's important to remember that creativity doesn't have to be about becoming a professional artist. For ESFPs, it's about self-discovery, finding joy, and expressing their unique perspective on the world. It's another avenue through which their natural brilliance can shine.

Channeling Chaos: Using Creativity for Problem Solving

ESFPs possess an incredible ability to see possibilities where others see limitations. Their adaptable nature, open mind, and preference for hands-on, experiential learning make them excellent problem-solvers, particularly when standard solutions fail. They bring a refreshingly playful and unconstrained approach that often unveils unique answers.

How ESFPs Approach Problem-Solving

Here's how the ESFP's creative mind tackles challenges:

- Big Picture Focus: ESFPs start by zooming out to get a sense of the overall problem and how all the pieces fit together. They're less concerned with granular details at the outset.
- Brainstorming Powerhouse: They love to throw out ideas, the more unconventional the better. There are no "bad" ideas at this stage, and they often build upon even the most outlandish suggestions.
- Connecting the Dots: ESFPs are remarkably talented at finding unexpected connections between seemingly disparate elements. This ability helps them come up with truly innovative solutions.

- Action-Oriented: ESFPs don't get stuck in endless analysis. They prefer to experiment, try different approaches, and learn from what works (and what doesn't).
- Social Intelligence Advantage: They naturally involve others in the problem-solving process. Their social charisma and ability to understand different viewpoints gives them access to a broader range of potential solutions.

When ESFPs Shine in Problem-Solving:

ESFPs excel in problem-solving situations that involve:

- Urgent Deadlines: Their ability to think fast on their feet and thrive under a bit of pressure makes them highly resourceful when time is of the essence.
- Creative Solutions Needed: When standard, tried-and-true methods aren't working, ESFPs inject new energy and a willingness to take calculated risks.
- Group Collaboration: Their infectious enthusiasm and ability to motivate others makes them natural group facilitators, encouraging everyone's input.
- "People" Problems: Their natural empathy helps them understand complex interpersonal dynamics. They are often the ones finding creative conflict resolution or mediating with grace.

Challenges for ESFPs

While they excel in many ways, here are some areas where they could use a bit more strategy:

- Easily Distracted: Their love of novelty can lead them down rabbit holes, potentially straying from the problem at hand. Staying focused can be a challenge.
- Finishing What They Start: ESFPs get excited starting new projects, but their attention can wane as solutions become clearer and the challenge is less enticing.
- Aversion to Details: Their preference for the big picture sometimes means important details fall through the cracks,

potentially causing future problems.

- Impulsivity: Acting before fully thinking things through can lead to hasty decisions.

Tips for Success

- Break It Down: Large problems feel overwhelming. Smaller tasks are less daunting.
- Collaborate: Find a detail-oriented partner to help ground their big ideas.
- The Accountability Buddy: Having someone to check in with keeps them motivated as the initial excitement wears off.
- "Good Enough" is Sometimes Enough: Perfectionism can prevent them from moving forward. Recognizing when a solution is "good enough" for the time being is an important skill to develop.

ESFPs bring a valuable and unique perspective to problem-solving. Embracing their creative strengths, developing strategies to manage their challenges, and surrounding themselves with supportive people who compliment their skills sets them up for success and creates fulfilling opportunities for their ingenuity to shine.

THE GROWTH MINDSET

Embracing Challenges: Turning Struggles into Strengths

ESFPs are often recognized for their natural optimism, resilience, and ability to see the bright side even in challenging situations. However, this doesn't mean they always find change or difficult circumstances easy. Like anyone, they can become stuck in fixed patterns or fall prey to a fear of failure that holds them back from reaching their full potential.

The key to unlocking continuous growth for ESFPs lies in adopting a growth mindset. A growth mindset involves the belief that abilities, intelligence, and talents can be developed through dedication and the right strategies. This stands in contrast to a fixed mindset, where people believe that their qualities are set in stone and cannot be significantly changed.

Unfortunately, ESFPs, with their desire to feel competent and loved, can sometimes unknowingly slip into a fixed mindset. This might manifest as:

- Avoiding Difficult Tasks: A fear of failure or looking incompetent can lead ESFPs to stick to what they know and avoid challenges that push them outside their comfort zone.
- Giving Up Easily: When faced with setbacks, they may be tempted to throw in the towel rather than persevere and learn from the experience.
- Sensitivity to Criticism: Constructive feedback might be taken personally, seen as an indictment of their ability rather than an opportunity for growth.
- Comparing Themselves to Others: Focusing on the successes of those around them can lead to discouragement and a belief that they will never "measure up."

Why a Growth Mindset Matters for ESFPs

A growth mindset fuels the ESFP's innate potential and helps them navigate the inevitable bumps along their life path. Here's why it's so important:

- Embracing Learning: ESFPs crave new experiences. A growth mindset transforms every experience, success or failure, into an opportunity to expand their skills and knowledge.
- Resilience in the Face of Setbacks: Mistakes become stepping stones rather than reasons to give up. A growth mindset fosters perseverance, crucial for long-term success.
- Greater Self-Confidence: Believing in their potential for growth allows them to face challenges with determination, building a strong foundation for genuine self-esteem.
- Motivation & Drive: A growth mindset makes them hungry for learning experiences, leading to a sense of internal fulfillment and direction.
- Achieving Their Full Potential: With a belief in their capacity for growth, ESFPs open themselves up to limitless possibilities and avoid self-imposed ceilings on what they can achieve.

How to Cultivate a Growth Mindset

Developing a growth mindset is a continuous effort, but even small daily shifts in thinking can yield big results. Here's an ESFP's toolkit:

- Reframe Failure: Mistakes are not proof of lack of ability; they are opportunities to learn and improve. ESFPs need to become experts at shifting their perspective.
- The Power of "Yet": Adding "yet" to self-judgments turns them into possibilities. Instead of "I'm bad at math," it's "I'm not good at math *yet*."
- Celebrate Effort, Not Just Outcome: Recognize the hard work and determination behind any outcome, not just whether it was a textbook "success."
- Seek Growth-Focused Feedback: Ask for constructive

criticism that points out areas for development and offers guidance on HOW to improve. This can take practice!

- Focus on Your Own Path: Comparison is the thief of joy. Celebrate the progress of others, and then refocus on YOUR personal journey and how far YOU'VE come.

Cultivating a growth mindset requires self-awareness, patience, and a willingness to confront uncomfortable feelings at times. However, the ESFP's natural curiosity and desire for fulfilling experiences provide fertile ground. The rewards of this shift in mindset are immense, both in terms of outward successes and the powerful sense of inner confidence knowing they are continuously evolving and capable of overcoming any challenge.

Lifelong Learners: The ESFP's Quest for Improvement

One of the most beautiful characteristics of ESFPs is their unquenchable thirst for new experiences. However, to ensure these experiences truly contribute to their personal development, it's important to combine that thirst with a growth-oriented perspective that embraces learning as a lifelong adventure.

Here's where a growth mindset shifts how the ESFP approaches learning:

- It's Not About Perfection: Learning isn't about achieving a flawless result immediately; it's about embracing the process of making mistakes, improving, and slowly building mastery.
- Focus on Progress, Not the Destination: ESFPs can become frustrated if their expectations for themselves don't match the reality of the learning curve. A growth mindset helps them celebrate small wins along the way instead of becoming discouraged by how far they still have to go.
- Learning Can Be Playful: For the ESFP, learning should be engaging and fun! When they find enjoyment in the process itself, they're far more likely to stick with it.
- Variety is Spice: ESFPs learn best through hands-on

experiences, experimentation, and a variety of formats. Dry lectures won't hold their attention as much as a dynamic workshop, an interactive project, or even learning through play.

- The Power of Community: Learning alongside others, sharing discoveries and collaborating brings added joy and motivation for the ESFP. They thrive on a sense of shared journey.

Here are some ways ESFPs can embrace lifelong learning with a growth mindset:

- Pursue Passion Projects: Pick up a hobby they've always been curious about, learn a new skill, or start a creative side-hustle. Learning is easier when they are truly excited about the subject!
- Step Outside Their Comfort Zone: Deliberately seek experiences that challenge them in new ways, whether it's a public speaking class, rock climbing, or learning a foreign language.
- Redefine "Success": ESFPs need a definition of success that emphasizes perseverance, effort, and the sheer joy of acquiring new knowledge.
- Find the Right Learning Style: Do they learn best by watching videos, listening to audiobooks, or attending hands-on workshops? Understanding their individual needs makes learning far more effective.
- Surround Themselves with Growth-Minded People: Seek out supportive friends, mentors, or communities that encourage their journey of learning and value the process as much as the outcome.

Important note: ESFPs can get caught in a cycle of starting exciting new things only to lose interest after the initial burst of inspiration. Here's the key to maintaining momentum:

- Start Small: Big goals are great, but start with realistic, achievable steps they can integrate into their daily or weekly routine.

- Set Short-term Milestones: Create a sense of accomplishment with small wins early on.
- Accountability Partners: Find a friend to check on their progress or a learning buddy who shares their goals.

A growth mindset gives the ESFP permission to try, fail, adjust, adapt, and persist in their pursuit of continuous self-improvement. As they embrace learning, not as a means to an end but as an endless source of joy and personal fulfillment, they tap into an ever-expanding version of themselves and unlock their boundless potential.

FINDING YOUR TRIBE

The Importance of Supportive Friendships: Seeking Your People

ESFPs are the social butterflies of the personality world. They bring warmth, enthusiasm, and a vibrant energy to any gathering. While they may have a wide network of acquaintances and generally enjoy the company of many diverse types of people, having a close tribe of supportive friends is essential for their overall well-being.

The right kind of friends offer ESFPs a crucial safe haven. They provide the space for them to be their fully authentic selves, recharge their social batteries when needed, and weather life's inevitable storms with a strong support network in place.

Here's why supportive friendships are especially vital for ESFPs:

- Emotional Validation & Acceptance: ESFPs deeply desire to be seen, understood, and loved for who they genuinely are. True friends offer this without judgment, celebrating their quirks, accepting their flaws, and encouraging their growth.
- A Place to Take Off the Mask: While ESFPs thrive in social situations, constantly performing can be exhausting. Close friends provide the space where they can let down their guard, be vulnerable, and know that they don't always have to be "on."
- Combating Loneliness: ESFPs can experience surprising bouts of loneliness despite their outgoing nature. Having friends they feel a deep connection with helps fill that internal void and provides a sense of true belonging.
- Sounding Boards for Growth: Trusted friends offer honest feedback, helping ESFPs gain self-awareness, and they encourage them to step outside their comfort zone for personal development.

- Amplified Fun & Joy: ESFPs find immense pleasure through shared experiences, laughter, and adventures with good friends. Their natural enthusiasm multiplies in the presence of those who truly "get" them.

Identifying Your True Tribe

Unfortunately, not everyone ESFPs encounter will have the capacity to offer them the kind of deep and supportive friendship they crave. Here's what they should be looking for in their inner circle:

- Shared Values: While superficial similarities can be fun for a while, deep friendships are formed on common core values and outlooks on life.
- Open Heart & Mind: ESFPs need friends who are non-judgmental, embrace their differences, and offer unwavering acceptance.
- Emotional Depth: While ESFPs love a good time, they need friends who can handle the full range of human emotion, offer empathy during tough times, and celebrate their successes.
- Reciprocity: Healthy friendships involve a balance of give and take. ESFPs need friends that will uplift and encourage them as much as they do for others.
- Growth & Adventure: ESFPs crave friends who share their curiosity about the world, who are always up for trying new things and pushing their own personal boundaries.

Challenges an ESFP May Face with Friendships

Even navigating friendships can have its complications for an ESFP:

- People-Pleasing Tendencies: Their desire to be liked and their ability to easily see things from others' perspectives can lead them to put their own needs last to try to please everyone.
- Losing Themselves in Relationships: ESFPs sometimes struggle with codependency in friendships, neglecting their

own individuality and needs in their focus on others.

- Sensitivity to Criticism: Due to their deep desire to be accepted, ESFPs may personalize feedback from friends or interpret concern as disapproval.
- FOMO Creates Conflict: Their spontaneous and adventurous nature can sometimes create friction if their friends don't share their same level of on-the-go energy.

Building deep, lasting friendships takes time, effort, and vulnerability. But for ESFPs, seeking those authentic connections that will stand the test of time is one of the most rewarding endeavors they'll embark upon.

Building Meaningful Connections: Beyond Superficial Bonds

ESFPs possess an undeniable ability to connect easily with a wide range of people. Their warmth and charisma naturally attract others. However, creating close, lasting friendships that provide them with the depth of emotional support they crave takes a bit more effort and involves a conscious approach.

Here are strategies for ESFPs seeking to cultivate deeper, more meaningful connections:

- Practice Vulnerability: Let down your guard and gradually share more of your true self with potential close friends – your fears, insecurities, and dreams, without the pressure to be endlessly upbeat.
- Ask Deeper Questions: Move conversations beyond the surface level. Ask about your friends' passions, life philosophies, or what brings them true joy. Show genuine curiosity about their inner world.
- Be a Truly Present Listener: Put away distractions and give your friend full focus. Ask follow-up questions to show you're engaged and demonstrate that you care about understanding their experiences.
- Offer Support Beyond Good Times: Be there for your friends during difficult times. Offer a listening ear, practical help

where appropriate, or just your presence without trying to solve their problems.

- Create Shared Experiences: Memories built together solidify bonds. Plan adventures, sign up for a class together, or start a fun tradition unique to your friendship.
- Be Reliable & Consistent: ESFPs sometimes overextend themselves or become swept away by the next exciting thing. Strive to show up for your friends consistently, follow through on your word, and put time into nurturing these important relationships.

Importantly, building meaningful friendships is a two-way street. ESFPs also need to:

- Set Healthy Boundaries: Learn to say no and communicate your needs clearly to friends to avoid people-pleasing or neglecting their own needs.
- Accept That Not Everyone Is "Tribe" Material: Some people are meant to be fun acquaintances, and that's okay. Don't force more intimate connections where they don't naturally fit.
- Practice Discernment: Choose your close circle wisely. True friends will celebrate your growth, support your dreams, and bring out the best in you.

Finding Where Your People Are

For ESFPs, a great place to start is by looking to their existing interests:

- Shared Hobbies: Joining clubs, classes, or groups related to your passions puts you in direct contact with like-minded people – fertile ground for new friendships.
- Volunteer Work: Serving a cause you care about is a great way to bond with others over shared values and make a positive impact at the same time.
- Online Communities: While they should never truly replace in-person interaction, online groups can be a good

place to connect with those who share niche interests or who understand specific life experiences.

Finding your tribe is an ongoing process. Some friendships will be deeply fulfilling for a season, while others provide a sense of belonging throughout different stages of life. Be open to new connections, trust your intuition about whether someone has true friend potential, and allow relationships to deepen organically.

The Rewards of True Connection

For ESFPs, investing in genuine friendships yields incredible rewards. Having that support system adds a new richness to their experiences, helps them weather challenges with resilience, and allows them to be more fully themselves, knowing they have people who love and accept them unconditionally.

NURTURING INNER BALANCE

The Art of Self-Care: Respecting Your Emotional Needs

ESFPs are often so focused on creating exciting and joyful experiences for themselves and others that they can easily overlook their own emotional and physical needs. Their natural inclination to put others first and their desire to avoid burdening anyone with their worries can lead to a detrimental pattern of self-neglect.

Self-care is an essential act of self-love for anyone, but it's especially important for ESFPs. It's about recognizing their own needs, honoring their limits, and ensuring they have the energy, clarity, and emotional balance to show up as their joyful, vibrant selves for both themselves and those they love.

Here's why self-care needs to become a priority for ESFPs:

- Avoiding Burnout: ESFPs run at a high energy level. Without rest and proper care, they risk mental, emotional, and even physical exhaustion. Their fuse gets short, their joy dampens, and they're less able to be the source of light they love to be.
- Preventing Resentment: When always putting others first, ESFPs might start to feel unseen, unappreciated, or even resentful. Setting boundaries and taking care of their own needs helps prevent this destructive buildup.
- Role Modeling: If ESFPs neglect their own well-being, it sends a subtle message to those around them that self-care is unimportant. They deserve to prioritize themselves and can model that for their children, partners, and friends.
- Enhancing Relationships: When they're emotionally balanced and well-rested, ESFPs have more to give in their relationships. They become better listeners, more engaged

parents, and more supportive friends and partners.

- Coping with Difficult Times: Self-care practices give ESFPs the resilience to handle challenges with more grace and strength. They don't deplete their emotional reserves as quickly.

Challenges the ESFP Faces with Self-Care

ESFPs may struggle to make self-care a priority due to several factors:

- Guilt: They feel a deep sense of responsibility for others' happiness, leading to guilt when they take time for themselves or say no to requests.
- Fear of Selfishness: ESFPs are so caring it can feel wrong to focus on their own needs – this is a misconception!
- "I'll Do It Later" Syndrome: Procrastinating on important self-care routines because they're caught up in the immediate moment.
- FOMO = Enemy of Self-Care: Fear of missing out drives them. When it feels like something fun is always happening, quiet time for rest seems like a waste.

The good news: Self-care doesn't have to be a boring obligation! Here's how to make it work for an ESFP personality type...

Saying "Yes" to Yourself: Finding Self-Care that Fits

The idea of sitting down for a quiet meditation session likely makes most ESFPs want to run in the opposite direction! They need a view of self-care that aligns with their vibrant personality and sensory-oriented way of experiencing the world. Otherwise, they'll likely rebel or feel forced and resentful. Here's how to make self-care work for an ESFP:

- Redefine Self-Care: ESFPs need to expand their view of what it means. It's not just bubble baths (though those can be nice!). Self-care for them is ANY activity that fills up their energy well, nourishes their soul, or helps them feel emotionally balanced.

- Focus on the Fun: Infuse self-care with a sense of play and adventure. A dance session in their living room, trying a new fitness class, or exploring a hiking trail all count!
- Engage the Senses: Activities that delight their senses are naturally rejuvenating. Enjoying time in nature, listening to uplifting music, getting a massage, or preparing a delicious meal can all be powerful acts of self-care.
- Mini-Moments Matter: Self-care doesn't require huge chunks of time. Short walks, a few minutes of journaling, staring at the clouds – small, intentional moments throughout the day add up.
- Make it Social: Sometimes the best form of self-care is connecting with loved ones. A laughter-filled afternoon with a close friend, a venting session with a trusted confidant, or a heartfelt conversation nourish the ESFP's spirit.

Areas Where Self-Care is Crucial for ESFPs

- Physical Well-being: ESFPs love moving and experiencing life through their bodies, but sometimes forget about the basics: getting enough sleep, eating healthy, staying hydrated, and scheduling in regular exercise (ideally, the kind they actually find fun!).
- Alone Time: This is HUGE for ESFPs. Even short periods of quiet time do wonders for their ability to reset, process thoughts, and just recharge their social batteries.
- Emotional Outlets: Find healthy ways to release pent-up emotions – creative expression, vigorous exercise, talking to a trusted friend or therapist, journaling – whatever works for them.
- Saying No: Learning to politely but firmly decline requests on their time or energy protects their emotional well-being and allows them to say "yes" to the things that truly matter.
- Embracing Imperfection: ESFPs hold themselves to high standards. They need to give themselves permission to be messy, make mistakes, and have days where they're just not

feeling their best.

Tips for Success:

- Schedule It: Put self-care on the calendar, even short 15 minute blocks, treating it as any important appointment they wouldn't miss.
- The Accountability Buddy: A friend to check in who helps them follow through on their self-care intentions can be invaluable, especially at first.
- Start Small: Big lifestyle overhauls are overwhelming. Choose one small self-care practice and build from there.

Self-care is a practice, not perfection. There will be days when ESFPs drop the ball. It's about self-compassion, adjusting the plan, and trying again. The more ESFPs prioritize their own needs, the more they have to give, both to themselves and those they love. True joy doesn't come from endless outward giving while running on empty. It comes from being so full of energy, love, and inner peace that it naturally overflows to those around them and enhances all their experiences in life.

HANDLING CAREER PRESSURES

Finding Fulfilling Work: Beyond the 9-5

ESFPs with their spontaneous spirit, love of variety, and natural focus on the present-moment, often struggle to find the right fit within traditional career paths. The idea of a rigid 9-5 routine, a job that offers little stimulation, or work that feels misaligned with their personal values can feel suffocating, leaving them unfulfilled.

The pressure to choose a "practical" or "stable" career path can come from various sources:

- Societal Expectations: There's often an underlying expectation that everyone needs a defined career path with a linear trajectory and a prestigious-sounding job title.
- Family Pressure: Well-meaning parents or family members may push ESFPs towards careers they deem "secure" or "responsible" even if they don't fit with their personality or desires.
- Comparison Trap: Seeing peers climbing career ladders or achieving conventional success can lead to self-doubt and a feeling of being "behind."
- Internal Struggle: ESFPs themselves often desire stability, financial security, and the feeling that they're making a meaningful contribution to the world.

This internal and external pressure creates a perfect storm. ESFPs want to find work they're passionate about, something that allows them to express their creativity, and lets them feel like they're making a difference. Yet at the same time, their desire for freedom, spontaneity, and flexibility may feel at odds with traditional careers.

Here's where ESFPs run into challenges in the workplace:

- Restrictive Environments: Offices with strict rules, repetitive tasks, and limited opportunities for creativity or collaboration can leave them feeling demotivated and drained.
- Boredom & Stagnation: If a job lacks challenges, opportunities for learning, or potential for growth, the ESFP will quickly start seeking stimulation and greener pastures.
- Lack of Meaning: ESFPs yearn to feel like their work makes a difference. If they can't connect to the purpose of their job, even if well-compensated, it won't feel satisfying.
- Feeling Undervalued: ESFPs want to work for companies and bosses that see their unique skills – their infectious enthusiasm, social intelligence, and adaptability – as genuine strengths.

The Importance of Finding the Right Fit

When ESFPs find a career that aligns with their natural strengths and deep values, they excel. This fuels their motivation, boosts their overall well-being, and leads to a deeply fulfilling and successful life. But that fit won't be found in any career guide or by copying anyone else's path.

The ESFP Entrepreneur: Turning Passion into a Paycheck

Entrepreneurship can be an incredibly satisfying path for many ESFPs. It offers the freedom, flexibility, and creative control they crave while allowing them to pursue projects that align deeply with their passions and make a genuine impact.

Here's why an entrepreneurial path is well-suited for the ESFP:

- Master of Their Own Destiny: ESFPs dislike being told what to do. As entrepreneurs, they call the shots, set their own hours, and shape their work around their strengths and priorities.
- Variety is the Spice: They can create businesses that provide a mix of challenges - problem-solving, collaborating with

others, bringing creative projects from idea to fruition.

- Impact Driven: Entrepreneurship allows ESFPs to build businesses focused on causes they care about or create businesses that reflect their unique values.
- Focus on Connection: Many successful businesses are built on genuine relationships. An ESFP's natural ability to connect with others is a huge asset in client relations, marketing, and team leadership.
- Never a Dull Moment: The entrepreneurial path is full of surprises, constant learning, and the need to adapt. This perfectly suits the ESFP's preference for spontaneity and ability to thrive under a bit of pressure.

Of course, choosing this path has its fair share of risks and challenges:

- Unpredictability: Income can be less predictable, particularly at the start, which can be stressful especially if the ESFP is the primary breadwinner.
- Lack of Structure: ESFPs will need to create their own structure and routines, which they might naturally struggle with.
- Facing the Inner Critic: Self-doubt and fear of failure linger for any entrepreneur. ESFPs need strong support systems and a shift towards a growth mindset.
- Wearing Many Hats: Entrepreneurs often do it all – the creative work, bookkeeping, customer service. ESFPs may need to outsource or partner up to tackle areas outside their strengths.

Tips for the ESFP Entrepreneur

- Start with Passion: Identify a business idea centered around something they are truly enthusiastic about – this sustains them over the long haul.
- Network & Build Community: Their people skills are an asset. Tap into potential mentors, collaborate with others, find fellow entrepreneurial souls.

- **Embrace Learning as They Go:** ESFPs don't need to know everything on day one. Be willing to acquire new skills on the job.
- **Outsource or Delegate:** Play to strengths! Trading services or hiring assistance for tasks they dread frees up their creative flow and time.
- **Focus on Sustainable Income:** Avoid the feast-or-famine cycle of many creatives by aiming for multiple revenue streams or recurring income options.

The entrepreneurial path is not for every ESFP. But for those willing to embrace the challenge, it has the potential to be an incredibly rewarding journey of self-discovery, continuous growth, and the freedom to create a life and career that fully honors their unique and effervescent spirits.

ESFPS IN LOVE

Thriving in Relationships: Finding the Right Partner

ESFPs bring immense warmth, passion, and a sense of adventure to their romantic relationships. They crave deep emotional connection but also need the freedom to be their authentic, spontaneous selves. Finding a partner who both supports their zest for life and appreciates their sensitive side creates a foundation for lasting and fulfilling love.

What ESFPs Look for in a Partner

ESFPs are often drawn to partners who offer a sense of balance and qualities that complement their own:

- Emotional Depth: While ESFPs love to keep things lighthearted, they need a partner who can navigate the full spectrum of emotions alongside them and with whom they can be vulnerable.
- Stability & Grounding Influence: ESFPs benefit from a partner who offers a dose of practicality and can help them stay grounded when their impulsiveness gets the best of them.
- Supportive & Encouraging: ESFPs thrive with a partner who celebrates their strengths, cheers on their dreams, and provides unwavering support during challenging times.
- Shared Sense of Adventure: A partner who embraces spontaneity, enjoys trying new things, and keeps life exciting is ideal for a happy ESFP.
- Intellectual Stimulation: ESFPs need a partner who can keep up with their quick minds, engage in lively debates, and expand their world view.
- Independence & Respect for Freedom: They can't thrive with clinginess or controlling behavior. A partner who trusts

them and allows space for their individuality is key for a healthy relationship.

Potential Challenges for ESFPs in Relationships:

Even with the right partner, ESFPs may need to navigate a few potential pitfalls:

- Fear of Commitment: Their independent spirit and desire for open-ended possibilities can make long-term commitment feel scary early in a relationship.
- Living in the Moment: ESFPs sometimes struggle with long-term planning or addressing practical aspects of being a couple – finances, where to live long-term, etc.
- Conflict Avoidance: To keep things harmonious, ESFPs may sweep disagreements under the rug, leading to issues festering and resentment building if left unaddressed.
- Need for Excitement: If a relationship feels stagnant, ESFPs get restless. It's crucial to keep things fresh with surprises, shared adventures, and trying new things to keep the spark alive.
- Sensitivity to Criticism: Due to their desire to be liked, ESFPs can take constructive feedback personally, putting them on the defensive and hindering healthy communication.

Creating a Thriving Partnership

For ESFPs, finding the right partner is just the beginning. Nurturing a fulfilling, lasting relationship involves:

- Open Communication: Learning to talk about difficult emotions constructively builds trust and avoids their tendency towards conflict avoidance.
- Balance Spontaneity with Planning: Strike a balance between spur-of-the-moment adventures and making some long-term plans together that honor both of their needs.
- Celebrating Individuality: Support each other's hobbies, friendships, and need for occasional alone time. This keeps both partners feeling fulfilled outside the relationship.

- Finding Shared Fun: Actively work to keep the spark alive with date nights, trying new things, and carving out time for relaxed connection amidst busy lives.

ESFPs can be incredibly loving, committed, and supportive partners. When they find someone who allows them to be fully themselves, encourages their growth, and shares their zest for life, the bond created is both powerful and deeply joyful.

Balancing Independence and Commitment: Love on Your Terms

While ESFPs value genuine connection and have immense love to offer, their need for freedom and occasional aversion to deep emotional discussions can sometimes complicate the path to happy, enduring partnerships. Here's how to navigate these complexities for long-term success:

Communication for Connection

ESFPs should strive to:

- Initiate the Difficult Conversations: Share fears and needs before they become huge problems. A partner can't read their mind.
- "I feel..." Statements: When addressing conflict, focus on expressing their emotional experience rather than blaming.
- Focus on Solutions: When raising a problem, have some possible solutions ready - this makes it less overwhelming for their partner.
- Practice Active Listening: Their partner deserves to feel heard too. ESFPs need to slow down, put away distractions, and truly absorb what their partner is saying.
- Choose the Right Timing: Don't try discussing heavy topics when they're tired or distracted. Carve out dedicated time.

What they gain from this is immense! Strong communication creates deeper trust, a sense of security for BOTH partners, and the ability to navigate inevitable challenges as a team.

Mastering Healthy Conflict

Conflict is a part of any relationship, but ESFPs thrive with these shifts:

- Change Their Perspective: Conflict doesn't have to be "bad." See it as an opportunity for growth and getting needs met by their partner.
- Seek to Understand: Instead of getting defensive, get curious about their partner's perspective. Even in disagreement, there's something to learn.
- Take Breaks as Needed: If they get emotionally flooded, agree with their partner to take a 20-minute break and calmly revisit the issue when cooler heads prevail.
- Compromise Isn't Conceding: ESFPs sometimes fear compromise means completely losing their way. It's about finding win-win solutions, keeping the big picture of relationship harmony in sight.

Balancing "Me" and "We"

ESFPs need to safeguard their sense of self within a committed partnership:

- Don't Lose Themselves: Maintain their interests, hobbies, and friend groups. Staying connected to who they are makes them better partners!
- "Alone Time" is Sacred: Schedule guilt-free time for themselves. This allows them to recharge and come back to the relationship with renewed energy.
- Openly State Needs: They shouldn't expect a partner to intuit when they need space or adventure. Being upfront avoids resentment.
- Encourage Partner's Independence: The healthiest relationships involve two whole individuals. Support their partner's need for their own time and growth.

It's a delicate dance, and even in fantastic relationships requires conscious effort from both people. Open communication, valuing individuality, and a willingness to grow together foster relationships where ESFPs feel both loved AND have the freedom to fly as they so naturally need.

PARENTING AS AN ESFP

The Fun-Loving Parent: Bringing Joy to the Family

ESFP parents are like a burst of sunshine in their children's lives. With their infectious enthusiasm, zest for life, and spontaneous nature, they create a childhood filled with laughter, adventure, and a profound sense of being loved and accepted.

Here's where ESFP parents naturally excel:

- Masters of Play: ESFPs turn the most mundane tasks into opportunities for fun. They create silly songs, invent imaginative games, and find joy in simple everyday moments.
- Champions of Exploration: They encourage curiosity, organize impromptu outings, and embrace a "let's try it!" attitude that inspires their children to engage with the world.
- Source of Emotional Warmth: ESFPs are naturally affectionate and shower their kids with praise, hugs, and heartfelt encouragement. Their children feel deeply loved and supported.
- Memory Makers: From epic birthday parties to silly holiday traditions, they create cherished family experiences that children remember long into adulthood.
- Acceptance & Encouragement: They celebrate their children's unique personalities, champion their dreams, and create a safe haven for them to be their authentic selves.

The unique energy and strengths ESFPs bring to parenting create a vibrant and unforgettable childhood for their little ones.

Potential Challenges for ESFP Parents

Of course, no parenting journey is without its bumps on the road.

Some areas where ESFPs might need to stretch their comfort zone are:

- Consistency with Rules & Discipline: Their natural flexibility and focus on fun can sometimes make it difficult to enforce consistent rules or follow through on consequences.
- Dealing with Strong Emotions: Children have tantrums, meltdowns, and complex emotions. ESFPs who prefer to keep things lighthearted may struggle to guide children through these storms.
- Overscheduling: Their desire to give their children every opportunity can lead to overbooked schedules, leaving little room for downtime for both themselves and their kids.
- Long-Term Focus: Living in the moment means ESFPs can miss the forest for the trees with childrearing. Saving for college, addressing behavioral issues early on, or the nitty-gritty practical side of parenting may not be their forte.
- Guilt Over Time Away: ESFPs crave adult connection, but sometimes feel guilty when they take time for themselves, assuming they should spend every waking moment with their children.

Luckily, ESFPs are adaptive and quick learners. By developing a few strategies and recognizing their tendencies, they navigate even the tougher parts of parenting with their signature positivity and unwavering love.

Nurturing Depth: Helping Children Develop Emotional Intelligence

While ESFPs infuse their homes with energy and joy, parenting also involves helping children build the skills to thrive. Developing emotional intelligence, handling tough situations, and learning the importance of responsibility alongside the fun are important aspects of their role.

Here's how ESFPs can excel in this area:

- Open Door for Emotions: Create a safe space for their

children to express the full range of feelings, positive and negative. Avoid dismissive comments like, "Don't be sad," even if their instinct is to cheer them up.

- Help Them Name It: Teach children vocabulary for their internal experience – angry, frustrated, disappointed, excited, nervous. This starts their journey of self-understanding.
- Model Healthy Emotions: ESFPs shouldn't hide their own vulnerabilities. Letting kids see them work through a tough day in a healthy way is immensely powerful for their own development.
- Stories & Play for Understanding: Use age-appropriate books, movies, or role-playing scenarios to explore complex emotions and discuss how to handle them constructively.
- Patience over Perfection: ESFPs themselves prioritize positivity. It's okay if children take a while to master emotional regulation. Focus on small steps of progress and offering support over time.

Balancing Fun with Responsibility

ESFPs will need to find ways to incorporate this without crushing their kids' spirits:

- Chores as Teamwork: Make chores less tedious with music, competitions, or turning them into a silly game. This teaches kids valuable life skills, but keeps a bit of their ESFP parent's joyful spin.
- Age-Appropriate Tasks: Young kids can match socks, teens can cook dinner one night. Start small and level up responsibility with age.
- Natural Consequences: Sometimes, this is the best teacher. If they forget their lunch, they go hungry a day. Less nagging for the ESFP parent!
- Praise the Effort: Focus as much on the child TRYING as the final outcome. This keeps them motivated as they gradually master new skills.

Finding the Right Support

ESFPs can't do it all alone. Here's where some outside help is beneficial:

- Lean on The Stable One: If their partner is a good planner, have them handle school forms, doctor appointments, and the practical minutiae.
- Family Routines: A visual chore chart or a set morning routine that doesn't require the ESFP's constant management keeps things running more smoothly.
- Parenting Resources: Books, articles, or even a supportive parenting group can give ESFPs tools and perspective they may lack naturally.

Importantly, ESFPs should never lose sight of their greatest strength as parents: their boundless capacity for love, connection, and making childhood an adventure. By supplementing their natural gifts with a few strategies and recognizing where to seek support, they raise emotionally intelligent, resilient, and joyful humans!

LIVING YOUR BEST ESFP LIFE

Embracing Your Strengths: Shining as You Are

ESFPs possess a unique and brilliant combination of strengths that, when fully embraced, allow them to live fulfilling and joyful lives. They have the extraordinary ability to make the ordinary feel special and sprinkle a dose of magic into both their own days and the lives of those around them.

Here's a reminder of the ESFP's superpowers and how they pave the way for a life well-lived:

- Infectious Enthusiasm: ESFPs approach life with a contagious sense of excitement and optimism. Their ability to find joy in the simple things and their willingness to try new experiences inspires others while enriching their own lives.
- Social Brilliance: They make friends easily and form genuine connections. Their ability to understand others on a deep level enriches their relationships, creates a sense of belonging, and offers them a powerful support system.
- Living in the Present: Focusing fully on the here-and-now frees ESFPs from dwelling on the past or excessive future worries. This allows them to savor moments of joy, both big and small.
- Creativity & Spontaneity: They see endless possibilities and aren't afraid to shake up routines. This leads to a life filled with exciting experiences, unexpected adventures, and a resilience to get through challenges.
- Warmth & Empathy: ESFPs care deeply about their loved ones, celebrate their triumphs, and offer unwavering support during tough times. Their ability to offer comfort and understanding strengthens their bonds and creates a beautiful sense of community.

While these strengths are truly gifts, sometimes shadows can obscure the ESFP's brilliance. Addressing certain tendencies creates balance for a happier and more fulfilling life journey:

- Fear of Missing Out (FOMO): Learning the power of "good enough" and occasionally saying "no" frees up their energy for what truly matters and protects them from burnout.
- Distractibility: Small steps of focus can be game-changing - setting a timer, finding distraction-free zones, prioritizing a few important tasks each day.
- Overextending Themselves: Saying "no" is an act of self-love! Their desire to please sometimes results in taking on too much.
- Seeking External Validation: Focusing on their inner compass rather than solely what others think protects them from disappointment and builds a strong sense of self.

Tips for an ESFP's Best Life

Here's how ESFPs can thrive and cultivate a life that feels authentic, joyful, and aligned with their core values:

- Nurture Your Inner World: While social interaction is oxygen for ESFPs, make time for self-reflection, journaling, or activities that soothe the soul.
- Surround Yourself with the Right People: Seek friends who support your growth, accept all of who you are, offer honest feedback with love, and whose positivity matches your own.
- Embrace Learning as Adventure: Pursue hobbies, passions, and experiences that stretch you. Even small steps of personal growth are incredibly fulfilling.
- Find Your Purpose: Don't just chase external markers of success. What fills your heart with meaning and allows you to contribute positively to the world?
- Celebrate Your Imperfections: You are always evolving. Let go of unrealistic expectations, forgive your mistakes, and laugh along the way!

The ESFP's inherent joy and vibrant spirit are assets to the world. By recognizing their gifts, addressing their natural stumbling blocks, and surrounding themselves with love and support, they set the stage for a life as extraordinary as they are.

Beyond the Spotlight: Finding Purpose and Fulfillment

ESFPs are often drawn to the bright lights: entertaining, connecting, and creating moments of joy for those around them. Yet, true fulfillment comes from discovering how their unique talents can make a meaningful and lasting impact on their community or even the wider world.

Here's where ESFPs can start the journey of purpose-seeking:

- Follow the Joy Juice: What activities leave you feeling deeply energized and excited even when you're tired? These hold clues into your deepest passions and values.
- Tap into the Hurt: What world problems make you angry, sad, or fill you with righteous determination to fix things? Anger is an important clue to where your heart lies.
- Service in Action: Volunteering in areas related to your passions gives you a tangible sense of how you can be of service and opens your eyes to new possibilities.
- Think Outside the Traditional Career Box: Your purpose doesn't need to be your job, but it should be an important part of your life. This could be through activism, creative projects, community building, or anything that feels aligned with your soul.
- Find Your Cause Crew: Connect with others who share your passion. Collective action amplifies your impact and makes the journey far more fulfilling.

How your desire for purpose manifests in the world is uniquely yours to discover. ESFPs have a powerful ability to inspire others, create real change, and advocate for the underdog. Don't underestimate the impact you can have when your natural warmth, connection skills, and creativity are directed towards a cause you deeply believe in.

Conclusion: The ESFP's Gift to the World

ESFPs, with your boundless enthusiasm, social brilliance, and ability to find joy in life's simple pleasures, you are a gift to the world. You remind us all to slow down, savor moments, and celebrate the beauty that surrounds us.

But your journey needn't stop there. While you will always be "The Performer," by embracing your vulnerabilities, seeking growth, and finding ways to express the full spectrum of your personality, you become an even more powerful force for good. As you build self-awareness, nurture strong relationships, and discover your unique passions, you unlock the key to living a truly fulfilling, impactful, and authentically joyful ESFP life.

By understanding your strengths and addressing your challenges, you become unstoppable. Your warmth, empathy, and zest for life ignite a spark in those fortunate enough to cross your path. Use your gifts wisely – connect deeply, spread joy authentically, and let your adventurous spirit guide you towards creating a life you adore and a world that is better because you were in it.